Manifest

Accountability Prayer Journal

To prove beyond doubt or question

Shametria Favors Richardson

This is no ordinary journal but a prayer journal that holds your faith accountable!

Belongs/Presented To:

____

Date: ________________________________

ISBN: 9781798404867

Accountability Contract

Starting today, I ______________________________ will submit to the will of God for my life. I know and believe God's plans for me are good.
I, ____________________, give myself permission to experience all He has for me. I will hold myself accountable and will pray with expectancy to position myself to receive all God has for me. I will pray without ceasing.
I, ____________________, will walk by faith and not by sight.
I will trust in the Lord with all my heart and lean not on my own understanding. I will take the unknown leaps of faith to experience manifestations from spiritual to natural.
I, ____________________, will pray until I see the impossible manifest before me!

Printed Name: ________________________________

Signature: ______________________________ Date: _______________

"Then He who sat on the throne said, 'Behold, I make all things new.' And He said to me, 'Write, for these words are true and faithful.' And He said to me, 'It is done! I am the Alpha and the Omega, the Beginning and the End. I will give of the fountain of water of life freely to him who thirsts.'"

Revelation 21:5-6 NKJV

CONTENTS

Dear Child of God,

It's about to go down! Oh yes, it's on, and I'm so excited for you! You've just signed your Accountability Contract, meaning you're ready to be strategic and intentional with your prayer life. The very first sentence in your contract states, "I will submit to the will of God for my life." This is vital before moving forward. The #1 key factor to an effective prayer life, is making sure you're praying God's plans for your life. This is where your relationship with God comes into play. As long as you're intimate with God, His desires will become your hearts desires and your prayers will be in alignment with His will for you. I hear you asking, how do I know if I'm praying correctly? Don't panic, the Holy Spirit will assist you by deciphering what will go up to God or not. Just pray.

Key factor #2, FAITH! "Now faith is the substance of things hoped for, the evidence of things not seen." Hebrews 11:1 NKJV. This journal is titled Manifest for a reason. I need you to stop settling for mediocre and start doing the work to experience extraordinary. You were created for so much more! The stars are NOT the limit. God created the stars, so of course He can go above and beyond that! The moment faith becomes your lifestyle the unbelievable starts to manifest. Now check this out…

Did you know it's your responsibility to pray without ceasing until every one of your prayers are answered?

Did you know it's your responsibility, to read and know the Bible to be sure you understand God's promises to you?

Did you know you could implement the Word of God in your prayers, to make your prayers even more effective?

Did you know once the Word goes out from the mouth of God, it cannot return to Him void? Oh yes! It's going to accomplish and prosper in the things in which it was sent.

So if you didn't know, you do now because I'm telling you. Now REJOICE because you've made the decision to hold yourself accountable. You've purchased this journal and will move forward applying the above tools to your prayer life. Soon you will see the impossible manifest before you!

Blessings and favor,

Shametria Favors Richardson
The Faith Coach

How to Guide

Hold yourself accountable by journaling your prayers and praying until every prayer is answered. Just because you don't receive an immediate response, doesn't mean the prayer won't be answered. It is your responsibility to keep track and pray without ceasing. I designed this journal in a way that fits you personally, yet provides some guidance as well. Make it your own so that you use it during daily prayer times.

This journal contains six sections, and each section contains spaces for 12 specific entries. You may use the sections by month or by topic. Topics may include finances, family, ministry or anything else that meets your needs. Each checklist page has a blank space for you to enter whichever way you want to use the journal. Follow the guidelines below to get the most from this journal, but listen to Holy Spirit and personalize it as well.

God's Answers:

God's answers to prayers are generally: Yes, No, and Not yet

YES * You should expect for God to answer yes, as long as you're praying the will of God for your life, and He's ready for you to have it. Your faith, expectations and actions will keep the yes's coming. Not only will He say yes, but He will go beyond what you could ever hope for or imagine. Thank God for the yes's!

NO * Prepare yourself for God to say no. He's our father and knows what's best for us. Thank God for the no's. You never know what He spared you from or what better thing He has in store for you. He already knows what lies ahead, good or bad. Remember He's the author of your life.

NOT YET * Your prayers not being answered when you want it, doesn't mean the answer is no. It could simply mean not yet. God will not give you anything you're not ready for. Thank God for that! You'd just mess it up or lose it. Remember His timing is perfect! He doesn't always come when you want Him, but He is always on time.

Prayer Checklist:

A checklist is provided for each section. Write the title of each prayer in one of the blocks and check off when answered. You'll use this as an overview to easily see what has or hasn't been answered.

Prayer Flow:

A – admiration: adore God, words from your heart.
C – confession: confess your sins and repent.
T – thanksgiving: thank God for who He is, has been and will be.
S – supplication: ask for what you desire; make your requests be known to God.

Supporting Scripture:

Support your prayer with scripture. Write out the scripture that speaks to your spirit and applies to each particular prayer.

My Thoughts:

As you write your prayers, journal your thoughts and any communication between you and God.

Scripture References

Remember, it is your responsibility to read the Word, understand it and utilize Scripture in the way it applies to you. Here are a few personal favorites to help get you started.

Abundance: "Now to Him who is able to do exceedingly abundantly above all that we ask or think, according to the power that works in us," Ephesians 3:20 NKJV

Anxiety: "Be anxious for nothing, but in everything by prayer and supplication, with thanksgiving, let your requests be made known to God; and the peace of God, which surpasses all understanding, will guard your hearts and minds through Christ Jesus." Philippians 4:6-7 NKJV

Focus: "So let's keep focused on that goal, those of us who want everything God has for us. If any of you have something else in mind, something less than total commitment, God will clear your blurred vision—you'll see it yet! Now that we're on the right track, let's stay on it." Philippians 3:15-16 MSG

Forgiveness: "If you forgive those who sin against you, your heavenly Father will forgive you. But if you refuse to forgive others, your Father will not forgive your sins." Matthew 6:14-15 NLT

Hope: "For I know the plans I have for you," declares the Lord, "plans to prosper you and not to harm you, plans to give you hope and a future." Jeremiah 29:11 NIV

Needs: "And my God shall supply all your need according to His riches in glory by Christ Jesus." Philippians 4:19 NKJV

Protection: "He who dwells in the shelter of the Most High Will remain secure and rest in the shadow of the Almighty [whose power no enemy can withstand]." Psalm 91:1 AMP

Strength: "I can do all things through Christ who strengthens me." Philippians 4:13 NKJV

Temptation: "Submit yourselves, then, to God. Resist the devil, and he will flee from you." James 4:7 NIV

Trust: "Trust in the LORD with all your heart, And lean not on your own understanding; In all your ways acknowledge Him, And He shall direct your paths." Proverbs 3:5-6 NKJV

Wisdom: "He who dwells in the shelter of the Most High Will remain secure and rest in the shadow of the Almighty [whose power no enemy can withstand]." Psalm 91:1 AMP

2019

January

S	M	T	W	T	F	S
		1	2	3	4	5
6	7	8	9	10	11	12
13	14	15	16	17	18	19
20	21	22	23	24	25	26
27	28	29	30	31		

February

S	M	T	W	T	F	S
					1	2
3	4	5	6	7	8	9
10	11	12	13	14	15	16
17	18	19	20	21	22	23
24	25	26	27	28		

March

S	M	T	W	T	F	S
					1	2
3	4	5	6	7	8	9
10	11	12	13	14	15	16
17	18	19	20	21	22	23
24	25	26	27	28	29	30
31						

April

S	M	T	W	T	F	S
	1	2	3	4	5	6
7	8	9	10	11	12	13
14	15	16	17	18	19	20
21	22	23	24	25	26	27
28	29	30				

May

S	M	T	W	T	F	S
			1	2	3	4
5	6	7	8	9	10	11
12	13	14	15	16	17	18
19	20	21	22	23	24	25
26	27	28	29	30	31	

June

S	M	T	W	T	F	S
						1
2	3	4	5	6	7	8
9	10	11	12	13	14	15
16	17	18	19	20	21	22
23	24	25	26	27	28	29
30						

July

S	M	T	W	T	F	S
	1	2	3	4	5	6
7	8	9	10	11	12	13
14	15	16	17	18	19	20
21	22	23	24	25	26	27
28	29	30	31			

August

S	M	T	W	T	F	S
				1	2	3
4	5	6	7	8	9	10
11	12	13	14	15	16	17
18	19	20	21	22	23	24
25	26	27	28	29	30	31

September

S	M	T	W	T	F	S
1	2	3	4	5	6	7
8	9	10	11	12	13	14
15	16	17	18	19	20	21
22	23	24	25	26	27	28
29	30					

October

S	M	T	W	T	F	S
		1	2	3	4	5
6	7	8	9	10	11	12
13	14	15	16	17	18	19
20	21	22	23	24	25	26
27	28	29	30	31		

November

S	M	T	W	T	F	S
					1	2
3	4	5	6	7	8	9
10	11	12	13	14	15	16
17	18	19	20	21	22	23
24	25	26	27	28	29	30

December

S	M	T	W	T	F	S
1	2	3	4	5	6	7
8	9	10	11	12	13	14
15	16	17	18	19	20	21
22	23	24	25	26	27	28
29	30	31				

2020

January

S	M	T	W	T	F	S
			1	2	3	4
5	6	7	8	9	10	11
12	13	14	15	16	17	18
19	20	21	22	23	24	25
26	27	28	29	30	31	

February

S	M	T	W	T	F	S
						1
2	3	4	5	6	7	8
9	10	11	12	13	14	15
16	17	18	19	20	21	22
23	24	25	26	27	28	29

March

S	M	T	W	T	F	S
1	2	3	4	5	6	7
8	9	10	11	12	13	14
15	16	17	18	19	20	21
22	23	24	25	26	27	28
29	30	31				

April

S	M	T	W	T	F	S
			1	2	3	4
5	6	7	8	9	10	11
12	13	14	15	16	17	18
19	20	21	22	23	24	25
26	27	28	29	30		

May

S	M	T	W	T	F	S
					1	2
3	4	5	6	7	8	9
10	11	12	13	14	15	16
17	18	19	20	21	22	23
24	25	26	27	28	29	30
31						

June

S	M	T	W	T	F	S
	1	2	3	4	5	6
7	8	9	10	11	12	13
14	15	16	17	18	19	20
21	22	23	24	25	26	27
28	29	30				

July

S	M	T	W	T	F	S
			1	2	3	4
5	6	7	8	9	10	11
12	13	14	15	16	17	18
19	20	21	22	23	24	25
26	27	28	29	30	31	

August

S	M	T	W	T	F	S
						1
2	3	4	5	6	7	8
9	10	11	12	13	14	15
16	17	18	19	20	21	22
23	24	25	26	27	28	29
30	31					

September

S	M	T	W	T	F	S
		1	2	3	4	5
6	7	8	9	10	11	12
13	14	15	16	17	18	19
20	21	22	23	24	25	26
27	28	29	30			

October

S	M	T	W	T	F	S
				1	2	3
4	5	6	7	8	9	10
11	12	13	14	15	16	17
18	19	20	21	22	23	24
25	26	27	28	29	30	31

November

S	M	T	W	T	F	S
1	2	3	4	5	6	7
8	9	10	11	12	13	14
15	16	17	18	19	20	21
22	23	24	25	26	27	28
29	30					

December

S	M	T	W	T	F	S
		1	2	3	4	5
6	7	8	9	10	11	12
13	14	15	16	17	18	19
20	21	22	23	24	25	26
27	28	29	30	31		

https://www.vertex42.com/calendars/2020.html

"For I know the plans I have for you" — this is the Lord's declaration — "plans for your well-being, not for disaster, to give you a future and a hope. You will call to me and come and pray to me, and I will listen to you. You will seek me and find me when you search for me with all your heart."

Jeremiah 29:11-13, CSB

Section One – Prayer Checklist for

____

☐	☐	☐
☐	☐	☐
☐	☐	☐
☐	☐	☐

Date:	☐
Prayer Title:	

Prayer:

Supporting Scriptures:

God's Answer:

My Thoughts:

Date:	☐
Prayer Title:	

Prayer:

Supporting Scriptures:

God's Answer:

My Thoughts:

Date:	
Prayer Title:	

Prayer:

Supporting Scriptures:

God's Answer:

My Thoughts:

Date:	
Prayer Title:	

Prayer:

Supporting Scriptures:

God's Answer:

My Thoughts:

Date:	☐
Prayer Title:	

Prayer:

Supporting Scriptures:

God's Answer:

My Thoughts:

Date:	☐
Prayer Title:	

Prayer:

Supporting Scriptures:

God's Answer:

My Thoughts:

Date:	☐
Prayer Title:	

Prayer:

Supporting Scriptures:

God's Answer:

My Thoughts:

Date:	☐
Prayer Title:	

Prayer:

Supporting Scriptures:

God's Answer:

My Thoughts:

Date:	☐
Prayer Title:	

Prayer:

Supporting Scriptures:

God's Answer:

My Thoughts:

Date:	
Prayer Title:	

Prayer:

Supporting Scriptures:

God's Answer:

My Thoughts:

Date:	☐
Prayer Title:	

Prayer:

Supporting Scriptures:

God's Answer:

My Thoughts:

Date:	☐
Prayer Title:	

Prayer:

Supporting Scriptures:

God's Answer:

My Thoughts:

"But those who wait for the Lord [who expect, look for, and hope in Him] will gain strength **and** *renew their power; they will lift up their wings [and rise up close to God] like eagles [rising toward the sun]; they will run and not become weary, they will walk and not grow tired."*

Isaiah 40:31 AMP

Section Two – Prayer Checklist for

____

☐	☐	☐
☐	☐	☐
☐	☐	☐
☐	☐	☐

Date:	☐
Prayer Title:	

Prayer:

Supporting Scriptures:

God's Answer:

My Thoughts:

Date:	☐
Prayer Title:	

Prayer:

Supporting Scriptures:

God's Answer:

My Thoughts:

Date:	☐
Prayer Title:	

Prayer:

Supporting Scriptures:

God's Answer:

My Thoughts:

Date:	☐
Prayer Title:	

Prayer:

Supporting Scriptures:

God's Answer:

My Thoughts:

Date:	☐
Prayer Title:	

Prayer:

Supporting Scriptures:

God's Answer:

My Thoughts:

Date:	☐
Prayer Title:	

Prayer:

Supporting Scriptures:

God's Answer:

My Thoughts:

Date:	☐
Prayer Title:	

Prayer:

Supporting Scriptures:

God's Answer:

My Thoughts:

Date:	
Prayer Title:	

Prayer:

Supporting Scriptures:

God's Answer:

My Thoughts:

Date:	☐
Prayer Title:	

Prayer:

Supporting Scriptures:

God's Answer:

My Thoughts:

Date:	
Prayer Title:	

Prayer:

Supporting Scriptures:

God's Answer:

My Thoughts:

Date:	☐
Prayer Title:	

Prayer:

Supporting Scriptures:

God's Answer:

My Thoughts:

Date:	☐
Prayer Title:	

Prayer:

Supporting Scriptures:

God's Answer:

My Thoughts:

"Though the fig tree should not blossom and there be no fruit on the vines, though the yield of the olive should fail and the fields produce no food, though the flock should be cut off from the fold and there be no cattle in the stalls, Yet I will exult in the Lord, I will rejoice in the God of my salvation. The Lord God is my strength and He has made my feet like hinds' feet, and makes me walk on my high places."

Habakkuk 3:17-19 NASB

Section Three – Prayer Checklist for

____

☐	☐	☐
☐	☐	☐
☐	☐	☐
☐	☐	☐

Date:	☐
Prayer Title:	

Prayer:

Supporting Scriptures:

God's Answer:

My Thoughts:

Date:	☐
Prayer Title:	

Prayer:

Supporting Scriptures:

God's Answer:

My Thoughts:

Date:	
Prayer Title:	

Prayer:

Supporting Scriptures:

God's Answer:

My Thoughts:

Date:	
Prayer Title:	

Prayer:

Supporting Scriptures:

God's Answer:

My Thoughts:

Date:	☐
Prayer Title:	

Prayer:

Supporting Scriptures:

God's Answer:

My Thoughts:

Date:	☐
Prayer Title:	

Prayer:

Supporting Scriptures:

God's Answer:

My Thoughts:

Date:	☐
Prayer Title:	

Prayer:

Supporting Scriptures:

God's Answer:

My Thoughts:

Date:	☐
Prayer Title:	

Prayer:

Supporting Scriptures:

God's Answer:

My Thoughts:

Date:	☐
Prayer Title:	

Prayer:

Supporting Scriptures:

God's Answer:

My Thoughts:

Date:	
Prayer Title:	

Prayer:

Supporting Scriptures:

God's Answer:

My Thoughts:

Date:	☐
Prayer Title:	

Prayer:

Supporting Scriptures:

God's Answer:

My Thoughts:

Date:	☐
Prayer Title:	

Prayer:

Supporting Scriptures:

God's Answer:

My Thoughts:

"And my God will liberally supply [fill until full] your every need* according to His riches in glory in Christ Jesus."

Philippians 4:19 AMP

* Every need means EVERY need – physical, spiritual, mental and emotional. No area of your life is exempt from God's gracious supply.

Section Four – Prayer Checklist for

____

☐	☐	☐
☐	☐	☐
☐	☐	☐
☐	☐	☐

Date:	☐
Prayer Title:	

Prayer:

Supporting Scriptures:

God's Answer:

My Thoughts:

Date:	
Prayer Title:	

Prayer:

Supporting Scriptures:

God's Answer:

My Thoughts:

Date:	
Prayer Title:	

Prayer:

Supporting Scriptures:

God's Answer:

My Thoughts:

Date:	☐
Prayer Title:	

Prayer:

Supporting Scriptures:

God's Answer:

My Thoughts:

Date:	☐
Prayer Title:	

Prayer:

Supporting Scriptures:

God's Answer:

My Thoughts:

Date:	
Prayer Title:	

Prayer:

Supporting Scriptures:

God's Answer:

My Thoughts:

Date:	
Prayer Title:	

Prayer:

Supporting Scriptures:

God's Answer:

My Thoughts:

Date:	☐
Prayer Title:	

Prayer:

Supporting Scriptures:

God's Answer:

My Thoughts:

Date:	☐
Prayer Title:	

Prayer:

Supporting Scriptures:

God's Answer:

My Thoughts:

Date:	☐
Prayer Title:	

Prayer:

Supporting Scriptures:

God's Answer:

My Thoughts:

Date:	☐
Prayer Title:	

Prayer:

Supporting Scriptures:

God's Answer:

My Thoughts:

Date:	
Prayer Title:	

Prayer:

Supporting Scriptures:

God's Answer:

My Thoughts:

"I will thank the Lord with all my heart; I will declare all your wondrous works. I will rejoice and boast about you; I will sing about your name, Most High."

Psalm 9:1-2 CSB

Section Five – Prayer Checklist for

____

☐	☐	☐
☐	☐	☐
☐	☐	☐
☐	☐	☐

Date:	☐
Prayer Title:	

Prayer:

Supporting Scriptures:

God's Answer:

My Thoughts:

Date:	☐
Prayer Title:	

Prayer:

Supporting Scriptures:

God's Answer:

My Thoughts:

Date:	☐
Prayer Title:	

Prayer:

Supporting Scriptures:

God's Answer:

My Thoughts:

Date:	☐
Prayer Title:	

Prayer:

Supporting Scriptures:

God's Answer:

My Thoughts:

Date:	☐
Prayer Title:	

Prayer:

Supporting Scriptures:

God's Answer:

My Thoughts:

Date:	☐
Prayer Title:	

Prayer:

Supporting Scriptures:

God's Answer:

My Thoughts:

Date:	☐
Prayer Title:	

Prayer:

Supporting Scriptures:

God's Answer:

My Thoughts:

Date:	☐
Prayer Title:	

Prayer:

Supporting Scriptures:

God's Answer:

My Thoughts:

Date:	
Prayer Title:	

Prayer:

Supporting Scriptures:

God's Answer:

My Thoughts:

Date:	
Prayer Title:	

Prayer:

Supporting Scriptures:

God's Answer:

My Thoughts:

Date:	
Prayer Title:	

Prayer:

Supporting Scriptures:

God's Answer:

My Thoughts:

Date:	☐
Prayer Title:	

Prayer:

Supporting Scriptures:

God's Answer:

My Thoughts:

"Worthy are You, our Lord and our God, to receive glory and honor and power; for You created all things, and because of Your will, they existed and were created."

Revelation 4:11 NASB

Section Six – Prayer Checklist for

____

☐	☐	☐
☐	☐	☐
☐	☐	☐
☐	☐	☐

Date:	☐
Prayer Title:	

Prayer:

Supporting Scriptures:

God's Answer:

My Thoughts:

Date:	☐
Prayer Title:	

Prayer:

Supporting Scriptures:

God's Answer:

My Thoughts:

Date:	
Prayer Title:	

Prayer:

Supporting Scriptures:

God's Answer:

My Thoughts:

Date:	☐
Prayer Title:	

Prayer:

Supporting Scriptures:

God's Answer:

My Thoughts:

Date:	☐
Prayer Title:	

Prayer:

Supporting Scriptures:

God's Answer:

My Thoughts:

Date:	☐
Prayer Title:	

Prayer:

Supporting Scriptures:

God's Answer:

My Thoughts:

Date:	☐
Prayer Title:	

Prayer:

Supporting Scriptures:

God's Answer:

My Thoughts:

Date:	☐
Prayer Title:	

Prayer:

Supporting Scriptures:

God's Answer:

My Thoughts:

Date:	
Prayer Title:	

Prayer:

Supporting Scriptures:

God's Answer:

My Thoughts:

Date:	☐
Prayer Title:	

Prayer:

Supporting Scriptures:

God's Answer:

My Thoughts:

Date:	☐
Prayer Title:	

Prayer:

Supporting Scriptures:

God's Answer:

My Thoughts:

Date:	☐
Prayer Title:	

Prayer:

Supporting Scriptures:

God's Answer:

My Thoughts:

About the Author

Shametria Favors Richardson is a personal faith coach, speaker and founder of Faith & Freedom Ministries. From her experience and gained knowledge, she learned once she understood faith she could operate in freedom. And once she was free, she could truly walk out faith.

It is her heart's desire to see believers around the world live in absolute freedom and establish an intimate relationship with God by applying faith-based principles to life, resulting in a full life transformation with faith and freedom.

About Faith & Freedom Ministries, Inc.

Make prayer, faith, and manifestations a lifestyle!
Keep your accountability journal in stock. Re-order through Amazon.com or at:

Faith & Freedom Ministries, Inc.
The home of
Shametria Favors Richardson - The Faith Coach
www.fafministries.com

To keep up with the latest news on all that GOD is doing
Follow The Faith Coach @
Facebook: Shametria Favors Richardson The Faith Coach
Instagram: Shametria_thefaithcoach

Do you desire unwavering faith, unshakeable trust or even a more intimate relationship with God?
How about the desire to live a life in absolute freedom?
If so, you need a faith coach.

Work one-on-one with The Faith Coach to uncover your specific path to freedom through faith in God. Together, we will explore the proven **FAITH 2 FREEDOM** Process to understand where you are today and how to create your personal path for a freer tomorrow.

BOOK THE FAITH COACH @
www.fafministries.com
Facebook: Shametria Favors Richardson The Faith Coach
Instagram: Shametria_thefaithcoach

53922880R10096

Made in the USA
Columbia, SC
23 March 2019